MERCY STREET

Anne Sexton

BROADWAY PLAY PUBLISHING INC
New York
www.broadwayplaypublishing.com
info@broadwayplaypublishing.com

MERCY STREET

© Copyright 2013 by Estate of Anne Sexton

All rights reserved. This work is fully protected under the copyright laws of the United States of America. No part of this publication may be photocopied, reproduced, stored in a retrieval system, or transmitted, in any form or by any means, electronic, mechanical, recording, or otherwise, without the prior permission of the publisher. Additional copies of this play are available from the publisher.

Written permission is required for live performance of any sort. This includes readings, cuttings, scenes, and excerpts. For amateur and stock performances, please contact Broadway Play Publishing Inc. For all other rights contact Brandt & Hochman, 1501 Broadway, #2310, NY NY 10036.

First printing: May 2013
Second printing: December 2013

I S B N: 978-0-88145-567-0

Book design: Marie Donovan
Page make-up: Adobe Indesign
Typeface: Palatino
Printed and bound in the U S A

INTRODUCTION
The History of MERCY STREET

The publication of Anne Sexton's drama, MERCY STREET, was a long time coming. A book of poetry, named closely after the play, entitled *45 Mercy Street*, made thematic and metaphorical reference to the dramatic version, and this book, posthumously published, was one of which my mother was proud. However, she felt ashamed of the play, which had been conceived and partially written some five years before, under the title TELL ME YOUR ANSWER TRUE at the Charles Playhouse in Boston.

Unfortunately, my mother later would direct that the play never be published or produced after its first run in New York City at the American Place Theatre in New York City in 1969. She wrote "Burn This!" across the title page of the manuscript, obviously desiring that no one ever see it again, either in print or on the stage. Her reaction was largely due to the reactions the play drew. She carried in her pocketbook a clipping of Walter Kerr's review from the *New York Times* until her suicide in 1974.

In retrospect, this review was not nearly so damning as she perceived it to be. Her reaction is testament to how fragile she had become about the play; a writer with a stronger ego might have considered it more of a "mixed review," because Kerr does note MERCY STREET'S "riveting line images," as well as her "striking use of ritual." His main complaint was that the play was "impotent to complete itself…a common enough failure in the theatre these days." He begins the review with the laudatory remark that she was "a fine poet with an astounding knack for incorporating the… immediate vocabulary of the pressing workaday world into lyrics that nevertheless remain lyrics."

Perhaps another part of her devastated reaction to the review was that MERCY STREET was unusually close to her heart, having been largely created at the Algonquin Hotel in New York City, where she lived for a time while watching the play develop on the stage and making last minute revisions, often quite extensive ones. During this time she made a note, dictated to a close friend and signed in her own hand that read this way:

"Writing is a solitary act. But at The American Place, I have found a community. One is not alone here. The work itself changes and becomes more vital as each day progresses. I have a feeling I never had before— that I have a family for my art. This is to be cherished beyond all things. Not alone. Together!"

As her literary executor, appointed just months before she died, I had followed many of her directions to the letter, especially the request that all her material be located in one archive, in one university, even though it would be much more lucrative to sell it off piece by piece. I complied with this request and placed all the material at the Harry Ransom Center at the University of Texas where the collections of many other well-known writers resided.

In went all of her papers, her manuscripts, her correspondences, as well as a plethora of such personal items as her typewriter, her reading glasses, much of her collection of books, including her thesaurus and her dictionary, and even her cigarette lighter, should the University ever want to mount an exhibition of the place where she created her work. But I did not burn the play, as she had directed. Conflicted, I instead put it away in a box beneath her desk cabinet, to be dealt with later. I reasoned that if she had really wanted it burned she would have done so before her death. Leaving it with her other papers seemed to me to express her ambivalence about destroying the work.

Yet, eventually I decided on a compromise: to send the manuscript of the play to Texas, under restriction. I arrived at the decision with the help and advice of her long-time editor at Houghton Mifflin, someone I trusted implicitly; he felt, and I agreed, that entire oeuvre should be represented, available to scholars some day in the future.

However, the restriction I made with the University was tight: no one would be allowed to view the play until I approved—perhaps until the death of my father, who was at that point only in his late fifties, and still vulnerable to all the revelations of my mother's life. No quotations from the play were ever to be allowed once I did approve. It seemed to me that such a restriction would enable me to change my mind if necessary. Not surprisingly, the university accepted the manuscript eagerly, even with the caveat in place, as part of her archive.

Over the years, I received many requests from scholars and students alike, all of whom wanted to study MERCY STREET as part of the body of her work. But I stuck to my restrictions, remembering her direction, written in a heavy hand on the manuscript: "Burn this!" This situation was a sharp disappointment to all those who wished to study the play, but I adhered to the decision I had made. People would just have to wait.

It is obvious, I think, that the compromise to place the play along with her other papers was not one made with ease. I was deliberately defying her wishes. But I had faced such decisions before and had sometimes decided to act against those requests, though in only a very few instances, just as I had adhered to them nearly explicitly in most others. There was some early poetry, the strained efforts of an immature writer who was just developing her voice, poems that had never seen publication, which she had also wished destroyed; these, too, went into the archive.

I felt that she had appointed me her literary executor for a critical reason: she trusted me to carry out her wishes, but she also trusted me to make new decisions when a situation warranted it. She could not have anticipated the clamor that would ensue when the play was denied to her scholarly audience. She could not have anticipated the desires of such individuals to study a very important chapter in her life and complete works, as she ventured into a genre new to her— drama—and to which she would never again return.

Three decades later, overwhelmed by such requests, I realized I now had to forge ahead in a different direction; it was a decision based on circumstances that were unforeseen at the time of her death. I considered for the first time opening the sealed box at the University. She had selected me—a daughter, a writer, one with whom she had shared her work for many years—rather than a friend or a compatriot in what she always called "this business of words." The situation was different than the one on which she had based her decision that I should burn the play.

Another factor led me to alter my opinion. I had, with further severe restrictions, allowed her biographer to study MERCY STREET as an important aspect of the life she was studying, to examine the many weeks that

my mother had spent in The Algonquin, working so
hard with the director and cast on this new adventure.
Her biographer was not allowed to quote or use any
material gleaned from the play without my express
permission as she read the text of many complicated
documents. This restriction seemed reasonable to
me because I retained such tight control over the
"forbidden" material, including also the notebooks
containing transcripts of her psychiatric sessions.

After the biography was published some ten years
later—to great fanfare, which resulted in an upsurge in
the studies of my mother's poetry—renowned scholars
and writers began to write to the biographer and me
regarding publication of the play, even though they
had not read it. Their entreaties were very persuasive,
and so, some thirty years after placing MERCY
STREET in her archive I began to consider opening the
sealed box that contained the manuscript of the play.
It took me a little bit more time, but eventually I gave
the University the written permission to allow scholars
whom I first approved to study the play.

Another nine years passed before Chuck Maryan,
the original director of MERCY STREET in New
York, wrote to me with the idea to publish it. Once
again, I remembered her instructions and once again
I considered yet another new situation that now
confronted me. The ensuing years since the opening
of the box had been filled with scholars who now
wrote to me regarding making the play available to
the public in a published form—even though it was
unlikely that it would ever be produced again. When
I consulted with writers and critics whose work I
admired and respected, I received a resounding,
unanimous reaction: all thought the play should be
published, though some did not want, and asked that,

their names not be used in an action that defied my mother's wishes.

When Chuck Maryan wrote to me, telling me that there was interest at Broadway Play Publishing Inc in publishing the play, I was still hesitant. However, eventually, in response to his well-reasoned plea, I finally agreed. In this way, at last, MERCY STREET comes to be published—and produced, should the opportunity ever arise.

Though I had finally fully defied my mother's wishes, I no longer felt torn. Rather, I was pleased, at last, to bring such an interesting and provocative work to her public. I believe, close to forty years after her death, that she would approve.

Linda Gray Sexton
Literary Executor
Estate of Anne Sexton
February 13, 2013

PREFACE

MERCY STREET was produced in October of 1969 at The American Place Theatre on west 46th Street in New York City. The theatre was, at that time, housed in Saint Clement's Episcopal Church, which was crucial to the realization of this play.

For those of us that participated in the development and ultimate production of this play, it was a landmark experience. Anne Sexton was always enchanting regardless of her state of mind. She had a definite talent for the theatre, something that she found hard to believe and she could and would rewrite without resentment. Anne attended every rehearsal and we all loved that she was there. She was always willing to answer our questions, no matter how intimate, as Daisy, the central character was Anne and the mother, father and great aunt were her family. The doctor was her psychiatrist at that time. Also, even though they were cut, over my protests, there were originally two additional characters called "The Witnesses". They were bizarre, hallucinogenic creatures, one shaped like an ear and the other was some kind of wizard. They spoke to Daisy and she to them. When I asked Anne if indeed she spoke with her demons that she saw she replied, "Yes, of course. I talk with them just as I talk with you."

The script came to me in a very different form than the one that opened in New York. Cindy Degener, Anne's agent, sent me the play and when I read it I thought immediately of The American Place Theatre, as it was dedicated to getting writers from other disciplines to write for the theatre. At that time they were having a great deal of success doing that. It turned out that they had already read the play and turned it down. However, I said, "Read it again and we will talk." They did and I convinced them to do a reading that I would put together after I had a phone conversation with Anne and received her permission to do so.

The first actor that I called was Marian Seldes. We had worked together in the past and I was able to call her directly. The conversation went like this:

CHUCK: Marian, I have a play by Anne Sexton.

MARIAN: I'll do it!

That was it. From that moment through the reading, the workshop, the rehearsal and a six-week run, Marian never wavered. She played Daisy, lent her spirit, talent and intelligence to helping us move the play from a talented first effort, by a poet, to a realized play for the stage.

Anne wrote MERCY STREET because she received a grant to write a play. Its original form set the play in a circus, with a ringmaster, and was in a magical, imagined place, where people could be called from the dead and the past could be revisited. It was theatrical but very confusing. However, what was clear for me was that this was a very American story about one generation passing its guilt and trauma to the next and culminating with the central character trying to decide whether to live or die.

The reading was successful enough to encourage the theatre to let us do an off-book workshop. This began a series of meetings between Anne and myself that went on over the course of the next year. We needed to find another environment for the play and one that would help unify the poetic language, with the many references to Christ, the revisiting of the past and the ultimate decision for the main character, Daisy, to choose between life or death.

We did the workshop and followed that up with the following decisions:

We set the play in an Episcopal church, during a Sunday morning service, a week before Easter.

The play would begin with Daisy seated in the audience and the authentic high Episcopal service would begin only to be interrupted by Daisy rising from the audience. This leads to the priest transforming into the psychiatrist and the sanctuary of the church transforming into the doctor's office, Daisy's home, with included various locales in the house.

At first glance, before the play began, the audience would see what appeared to be a traditional church setup. However, the set designer cleverly had the furniture built so that it resembled what one ordinarily saw in church, but it would not have, for instance, an armrest allowing it to become Daisy's bed, etc. Also as we had the stained glass windows, the lighting designer was able to light the windows from the outside, so that we always had bright sun to begin and end the play.

In putting the play together Anne and I went to church, sometimes together when I went to Weston. Or I would go on my own to Saint Mary's on West 46th street, the only high Episcopal church in New York City. We learned the steps of the mass, with some coaching by Episcopal priests, and found the appropriate music for that service. This music was then interlaced into the production by the Music Director of Saint Mary's so that one had the sense that the service was going on while Daisy was making her decision about her life.

The use of transformations was really the key to this production. The designers transformed the church to a doctor's office, a home with various bedrooms and then back again to a church. The actors transformed the set pieces into desks, chairs, beds, etc. and with few exceptions most of the props were created or mimed by the actors. However, everyone involved needed to be very specific about each locale.

Finally, this play was an experience that bound all participants in a very joyful way. It was a two year process and until Anne left us, I would see her every time that I was in the Boston area and we frequently spoke by telephone. I had hoped that Anne would write another play. She said she was too busy with her poetry. However, she did collaborate on an opera, which, curiously enough, I directed in New York in 1996. The title of the opera is "Transformations."

Charles Maryan
New York City
2012

MERCY STREET premiered at The American Place
Theatre (Wynn Handman, Artistic Director) in
New York in October 1969. The cast and creative
contributors were:

DR ALEX ....Jerome Raphel
DAISY ....Marian Seldes
JUDITH..Virginia Downing
AMELIA ....M'el Dowd
ARTHUR .... William Prince
ACOLYTES ...... Robert Bass, Chris Kalfayan, Paul Leavin,
Fritz Stokes

Director .... Charles Maryan
Scenery & costumes ....Douglas Higgins
Lighting.. Roger Morgan
Special sound ....James Reichert
Music selection & arrangement................McNeil Robinson

CHARACTERS

MALE ACOLYTES
PRIEST, *who is* DR ALEX, *psychiatrist*
DAISY CULLEN
JUDITH, DAISY's *mother*
AUNT AMELIA, DAISY's *great aunt*
ARTHUR, *(Ace)*, DAISY's *father*

MERCY STREET

(Church bells ring as audience comes in. Processional enters house right. Daisy *sits audience left. Processional goes center stage.)*

Dr Alex: Almighty God, unto whom all hearts are open, all desires known, and from whom no secrets are hid; Cleanse the thoughts of our hearts that we may perfectly love thee. Amen. Hear what our Lord Jesus Christ saith. Thou shalt love the Lord thy God with all thy heart, and with all thy soul, and with all thy mind. This is the first and great commandment. And the second is like unto it; thou shalt love thy neighbor as thyself. On these two commandments hang all the Law and the Prophets.

(Tape: Choir singing Kyrie Eleison*)* Lord have mercy upon us.

Daisy: *(She approaches stage.)* Christ have mercy upon us.

Dr Alex: Lord have mercy upon us. The Lord be with you.

Daisy: And with my soul.

Dr Alex: I believe in one.

Daisy: The Father Almighty, Maker of heaven and earth, and of all things visible and invisible. And in one Lord Jesus Christ, the only begotten Son of God; Begotten of His Father beyond all worlds, God of God, Light of Light, Very God of Very God, Begotten, not made.

Dr Alex: The Lord be with you.

DAISY: I most humbly beseech thee.

DR ALEX: To comfort and succour.

DAISY: All those who are in trouble.

DR ALEX: Sorrow and need.

DAISY: Or any other…

DR ALEX: Ye who do truly and earnestly repent of your sins draw near and take this holy sacrament.

DAISY: *(Cross, kneel right platform)* Almighty God, Father of my Lord Jesus Christ, Maker of all things; acknowledge and bewail my manifold sins and wickedness. Have mercy upon me, have mercy upon me, most merciful Father.

DR ALEX: Daisy, the body of Christ. Daisy, the blood of Christ. *(Offers sacraments, withholds them)·*Daisy, the body of Christ.· Daisy, the blood of Christ. *(Eats wafer and drinks wine, then crosses down center)*

DAISY: Am I to walk forever from breakfast into madness? Where is a supper I may take? Christ? Where is my Christ? Daisy Cullen. My real name's Amelia. I am a wife. A mother. I have three children. My daughter Abigail is thirteen. She's the eldest. My God, I hear the snuffling of the brown rats. They are waiting for me. I live in Cochituate. That's a little west of Boston. I am covered with dollar signs. I am looking for a ten-foot crucifix. It will burn like applewood, with splinters for each thumb. I am lost. No, I am Daisy. But Christ? You are Christ, hooked to your own weight? Christ?

DR ALEX: Daisy.

DAISY: The only one I'll talk to is Christ.

DR ALEX: Be seated Daisy Cullen. Now we shall proceed to unlock you from your Christ. I am the surgeon of the psyche, and I have a swift hand. Not delicate, Madam—accurate, precise! …Your attention, Madam!

DAISY: 100, 99, 98, 97, 96, 94, 93…

DR ALEX: You will watch…you will remember.

DAISY: No, Take them away.

DR ALEX: I'll breathe your past back into you mouth to mouth.

DAISY: Yes.

(Sound [CHOIR] I believe in one God, the Father Almighty, maker of heaven and earth)

DR ALEX: *(Crosses left to pulpit)* Begin.

JUDITH: Oh, it' s so divine, I've been called at last. Oh, how must I look? Such a frazzle. Everyone said I had lovely hair, an interesting nose, eyes…eyes like a cat—two colors. But now…who knows? Oh, I know, you think I'm just a self-absorbed menopausal woman but there was more to me…to my life…than that. I remember so much…lobsters at Monhegan, the little mare I had when I was ten; I remem ber best the sound of children at night before dinner. Just as Ace was mixing us both a martini there was that sound… the sound of children before dinner. At six o'clock every one calling names out across the neighborhood… even…even Daisy, who was usually only in the apple tree beside Aunt Amy's window. She'd call back to me, "Coming Mama", echoing back to me over the suburban lawns, over the neighbors' fences, all up and down the street, the little trusting voices.

DR ALEX: Enough Daisy's mother.

(AMELIA enters right.)

AMELIA: I come from a long line of Loveworthys who settled Massachusetts Bay Colony. I'm a lady. I demand to be treated with respect. I have a right. I dread this show. It's managed incorrectly. I don't have the slightest desire to live any of it over again. This whole place is like a badly designed machine…all this energy for no purpose.

DR ALEX: Enough Daisy's Aunt.

AMELIA: I say I ought not be put in jeapordy of my soul a second time for the same cause.

DR ALEX: Who says it's the same cause?

AMELIA: You told me Daisy would come in with an overdose of sleeping pills. Although safe in the hospital…pills, you said, she'd sewn them into the lining of her coat.

DR ALEX: Be seated Amelia Loveworthy.

(ARTHUR *enters up left.*)

ARTHUR: Well! Well! What's this! God! Wonder who it is? Could be dozens of people, I died so young, you know. Fifty eight is young these days. Could be any number of people who need me here…why I could name plenty. I was always a happy man. Though, I remember when Judith died, one year before I did, I didn't care much about living. No, sir. Couldn't even sell then. I was a salesman. Best damn one in the business. People believed in me. They said, "Ace Meredith has an honest face!" …I remember one gentleman, if you could call him that, with some of the deals he used to pull, deals, believe it or not, with high men in government, men right next to the President! …that man, we often ran into him at the Latin Quarter back in the days when I used to drink a little…God, it's wonderful to talk again… Well, this man, Benny, was his name, bet he's in jail by now, the way he used to give payoffs and mink coats and vacations in Jamaica to the President's left hand man…because of the tax bite, and believe me that tax bite was pretty rough in

our bracket…Benny used to come up to our table and
say to me, "Well, well, if it isn't Ace Meredith—to
know him is to love him!" …That's the way I was, I
could sell anyone, an honest face. Sell the buyer on
yourself, I always said, and get to the product later. It
wouldn't have mattered what the product was, I could
have sold it… Or so Judith used to say. And then, you
know, when she went that way I felt so damn empty!
I had always thought I could live alone. Women were
always attracted to me; my hair wasn't too gray; I used
to dye it…not actually dye it, but a little black stick you
rub on the edges… Oh, I hope I'm not boring you with
all these details. It's just the words piled up in my head
all these years… Well, Then Judith died…and then
I had a stroke and then, well…there wasn't anyone
to come into the living room to say, "Ace, remember
when?" …And my daughter, Daisy, she was still
sick and I felt sorry for her then. I told her right then
that I was sorry that we'd said she could go to a state
hospital for all we cared. When she first got sick I hated
her for it…her and her fancy psychiatrist. Angry, I
was . I'd just had a hemorrhoid operation and then she
flips. Told her what she needed was a good kick in the
you-know-what. Strange to have your own daughter
go crazy. Must have inherited it from Aunt Amy. I felt
sorry for her in the end…and that's the truth.

DR ALEX: In your place, Daisy's father.

(ARTHUR *sits left stool.*)

CHOIR; *(Tape)* Who for us men and for our salvation,
came down from Heaven and was incarnate, by the
Holy Ghost of the Virgin Mary and was made man.

DR ALEX: Straight into the crisis, Daisy. Plunge into the
middle of it.

DAISY: But Christ! Where is Christ?

DR ALEX: I don't allow that here.

DAISY: But I want to see Him.

DR ALEX: We're running late. Daisy, think back over your life and pick, quite at random, some scene for your one remembrance scene. Some scene that was beautiful, but tense…a time that made life seem more real, yet close to death. It must be a recent scene and yet one of no importance… A scene that comes readily to mind.

DAISY: Not Christ?

DR ALEX: No. Not Christ…a common seeming time.

DAISY: Not rocking the baby, for although children three, I have left everyone. Oh Christ, take care of them somehow…

DR ALEX: No time for that, here.

DAISY: Last July when my daughter Abigail won a silver cup at the horse show.

DR ALEX: Stop digressing.

DAISY: That year my husband shot three hundred eighty-nine squirrels from the bedroom window. He kept a perfect count. I would wake up at six o'clock and there he would be kneeling at the window aiming at the trees…and when they were dead he put them in the garbage pail. He hated my sickness. And the children would come to me and ask me, "Mummy, what's wrong with squirrels?" …You know…

DR ALEX: That will be enough foolishness.

DAISY: Not that clock I broke, oh when was it that I broke that clock… Awfully important, breaking that clock…

AMELIA: When she was ten she broke my clock, touched its hands, set it out of time. She hurt time! She had no right! The clock of my father that he bought in Genoa when I was a child. I was so angry with her—

only time I ever struck her in the face… But it was
mine! My own cuckoo clock. Little brown direct thing,
little brown, good little erect-thing, brown sound…
cuckoo, cuckoo…in and out…my prayers going back
and forth, my little counter down of all the hours…
And she set it out of time!

DR ALEX: I suggest that your body be important. What
about pain, and there's always sex. Eyes, shoulders,
breasts.

DAISY: Oh, I was sexy enough.

DR ALEX: Well! We're very short on time.

DAISY: No wonder I hated clocks…time was always
running down: the clock was always using itself up.

DR ALEX: Have you your scene?

DAISY: *(Crosses center)* Yes, I think I have a time as all
that…I had on a black dress that night in Venice, and
heels. Venice—the warehouse of the ages. My husband
and I were there last June. I was reading Aunt Amy's
Venice letters—a big, heavy volume bound in Morocco
leather—I took them with me to the bar. Really,
I'd never read those letters before although thirty
years ago she gave me her name…and when I was
bequeathed the letters she'd given up, dead, poor ghost
of herself… When she was in Venice it was way back
to 1889. But that summer when I looked in the mirror
in the hotel I looked just like her. I thought, I'm losing
me! …A picture within a picture…namesakes with the
same face.

AMELIA: With hair like that—never!

DAISY: Once I used to think she died in a fire, but that
was foolish.

AMELIA: *(Stands up)* I did—the fire you lit under me;
the fire of disgust!

DAISY: But I wasn't her really. I was living the wrong life for it. I pretended in Paris. In Paris I walked her walks, but that was over.

AMELIA: In ·those shoes! Never!

DR ALEX: Be specific, Daisy. What happened? Remember, you had on a black dress?

DAISY: I put it on just for him. We'd just made love. It was rather poetic, the way it happened. He came when all the bells of Venice rang.

AMELIA: Avert your eyes, child!

DAISY: I told him we'd start a new vogue with that as they did with the coins in the Trevi Fountain…and when we dressed, black dress, black shoes, white bag, white gloves.

AMELIA: A little late for gloves!

DAISY: And went to Harry's bar, a very American bar in Venice where they make real martinis. And, of course, I took the letters… Each day I'd been looking for her, going out across that Venetian facade, that stage set…looking for her as some people look for love in an amusement park. I needed to wear her life—to enter her death…

AMELIA: Death!…The death I held in my hands, the love that went out of me when he was gone…I could not cry for the dead as they did in the Great Plague of 1348 when the boatmen cried, "Any dead bodies?" … No, I was silent, holding my heart like a skull in my hands.

DAISY: At Harry's we had four martinis and then we ate and then…then the letters were gone…stolen…the space on the bar where I left them…was empty.

AMELIA: *My* letters on a common bar—martinis, revolting! Revolting Americans in a revolting American bar!

DAISY: My hands sucked dry by a thief… It was over then. I'd been riding a horse and was thrown. All of it gone, paragraph by paragraph… You see, at each bridge I had thought, "Aunt Amy, I'm here too—at your footprint!"

AMELIA: Hogwash! How could she know my footprint, how I walked alone up and down, over the little bridges, past the perenial merchant, past the Germans and Americans…alone… The man I loved, married. He belonged to someone else. How could she know in her little American bar how I stood alone gazing into the sunstruck canal?

DAISY: I started to cry, but he said he'd snap me out of it. *(Crosses down right)* We took a gondola ride. It cost three thousand Lira. We slipped through the inky canals, wrapped as in a corn husk, sleek and wet as a sleeping bat, down the side canals, watching the houses repeat themselves, under kitchens, and bedrooms… We lay together, side by side like children.

AMELIA: I hate you!

DAISY: *(Crosses center)* And then we walked over to the Piazza San Marco and they were having their Sunday night band concert. The tables were full so full so we stood on the side and listened. I took off my heels and we stood in the dark listening to *Pine De Sol* by Respighi and I cried. He said, "Daisy, do you realize you are standing in pigeon shit?"

AMELIA: Truck drivers talk! Alley talk!

DAISY: I didn't give a damn I told him! I was thinking how Aunt Amy stood there once and listened to just the same music.

AMELIA: Fool! That hadn't even been written then.

DAISY: Between songs I ran up to the band leader to thank him but he didn't understand. "Foolish Daisy!" my husband said, and I told him that my Aunt Amy could speak seven languages!

AMELIA: Wrong again! I spoke six and all *fluently*.

DAISY: Her family were advanced for the time. They spent half their time in Boston and half the year in Rome.

AMELIA: A prominent family—of ship builders and bankers—not salesmen!

DAISY: When the music started again he whispered "Have you got the black pants on" and then he patted my fanny. He meant was I dressed for love!

AMELIA: Standing there with her shoes off… It's sordid! How can she so despoil what I was?

DAISY: Black pant he wanted to know and there I was crying for Aunt Amy. I kep thinking, *Aunt Amy, Aunt Amy, I'm you! I'm really you!*

AMELIA: Daisy! Stop! Daisy, you couldn't know, you couldn't possibly know!

DAISY: (*Crosses to* AMY) Aunt Amy…Aunt Amy! Thank God, it's *you*. It's truly *you*!

AMELIA: Stop, foolish girl. Stop hurting me this way. I feel like a coat that you wore two seasons and then threw away because it went out of style.

DAISY: Aunt Amy, please…please!

AMELIA: I'm not just some guilty Victorian character out of your past. You used me…letting your life run over me like a runaway horse… You can't hang me up on the wall and smear black paint all over my face as you've done. Furthermore, I'm not like a statue of the Virgin either.

(Sound: bells)

AMELIA: Why don't you stop playing ghosts! Since you seem to have hung me up in your mind so firmly ever since I died—a poor old lunatic woman—

DAISY: Me, too, Aunt Amy—a crazy lunatic woman!

AMELIA: No one is a lunatic *here*. There is no room for such things, And further, since you've hung me up in your mind like a Virgin you had better understand what kind of a virgin I was and further, why! You couldn't have any comprehension of the word. As soon as you became aware of your maidenhood you offered it up to your father like a piece of chocolate.

ARTHUR: Shut up, for God' s sake, make her shut up! *(He exits left.)*

JUDITH: She's crazy: don't listen to her.

DAISY: Christ come back to me. I' m calling to you. Look down from your tree of nails and speak to me.

DR ALEX: Enough. Back in your places.

CHOIR: *(Tape)* And He shall come again with glory to judge both the quick and the dead.

DR ALEX: Daisy, Judith, Arthur, Amelia, that series of events that changed you.

DAISY: No event, no event at all…no fire, no desire.

CHOIR: *(Tape)* Whose Kingdom shall have no end.

DR ALEX: Daisy, your attention, please, we will begin. You are now thirteen. You menstruated for the first time last month. Now your father is in the basement cleaning his skeet guns, nipping on some black market Scotch.

(JUDITH sits on chaise.)

DR ALEX: Your mother is on her chaise longue icing her wrists and her forehead.

(AMY *at prie-dieu right*)

DR ALEX: Your Aunt Amy has been balancing her checkbook and listening to the market reports; she will speak with your mother for a moment and then return to her study to tear up her stock certificates.

(DAISY *sits center with back towards audience*)

DR ALEX: You are playing jacks and singing. (*Out down center*)

DAISY: HEY, DADDY, I WANT A BRAND NEW CAR, CHAMPAGNE, CAVIAR, HEY, DADDY, YOU WANT TO GET THE BEST FOR ME, DE-AH, de-ah, de-ah, de-ay…

(AMY *crosses to* JUDITH's *room.*)

AMELIA: Judith, I must speak to you. It can't be allowed to continue in this fashion.

JUDITH: What can't be allowed?

AMELIA: Your financial position. It's time *you* were aware of it!

JUDITH: Ace handles all that, dear. You know very well that I flunked math all through school.

AMELIA: It's. time you knew a few small facts about money.

JUDITH: The doctor said you'd have to go away for a rest if you kept talking about money. Money or the Bible. You're sick on both subjects. You have moments you're not yourself. *Now* you're the accountant… *Next* you'll be the minister.

AMELIA: Poppycock! I know what I'm talking about. This house, for instance, you're aware that I bought it for you. Thirteen years ago I bought it for you outright!

JUDITH: An investment, you said, The Cliff Estates in Wellesley are an investment, you said.

AMELIA: An investment, not only in real estate—an investment in a family…I wanted to belong to you.

JUDITH: And Daisy had just been born.

AMELIA: And Daisy is just what I wanted.

JUDITH: Ace said it would be good for us to have you live with us; good for the baby, good for me. But he was thinking about *you* when he said it.

AMELIA: I had a career, a position, but you had a child.

JUDITH: This has been your home for thirteen years. Daisy is your namesake… What has all that to do with finances?

AMELIA: In thirteen years I've spent two hundred fifty thousand dollars. Out of capital!

JUDITH: On what, for God's sake?

AMELIA: On Arthur, you fool!

JUDITH: Ace doesn't need your money!

AMELIA: I have given my last cent to that man, I haven't *loaned* it! I've *given* it!

JUDITH: He doesn't need your gifts!

AMELIA: This past year I've sold five hundred Detroit Edison, three hundred American Tel and Tel, one hundred Northern Pacific, and twenty American Can.

JUDITH: Don't come in here like some accountant!

AMELIA: It's gone, Judith, down the sink hole on a weak man, as weak as your father.

JUDITH: Daddy wasn't weak. He got a bad break.

AMELIA: You call that foolhardy stock market tip a bad break? I wasn't that foolish with my investments.

JUDITH: No, you were silent. Miser!

AMELIA: We started out with the same investments, your father and I. But during the First World War he was too greedy, gambling it all away on wheat futures in the Chicago grain market.

JUDITH: Why talk about it anymore? Can't you hear Daisy singing out there?

AMELIA: Yes, I hear my little namesake. She's the only innocent one left in this world.

JUDITH: Go to *her* then. Don't hurt *me* with stories of daddy.

AMELIA: Don't you know that your father squandered a fortune—even then. Even then a weak man could do it!

JUDITH: Go back to your knitting!

AMELIA: Back to my knitting so you can think of your father as some editorial giant at the newspaper, as the rider of horses, the sailor of boats. Back to my knitting so you don't have to look your father...*or* your husband in the eye!

JUDITH: Please God Damn it! Shut up!

AMELIA: And now you're rude!

JUDITH: But daddy...oh, I can't bear to think of daddy that way...broken and lost.

AMELIA: I'll be broken and lost myself if I continue to put good money after bad. I can't afford the luxury of supporting *this* family, too.

JUDITH: Liar! Liar!

AMELIA: You have possessed my checkbook and have covered me with debts and lies.

JUDITH: Crazy talk, You're not yourself. You never supported us. Daddy was different, You bailed him out.

AMELIA: And Ace never said I bailed him out?

JUDITH: Certainly not!

AMELIA: It's. time you asked *him*.

JUDITH: Crazy talk. Ace Meredith! He never lost anything in his life!

AMELIA: You believe, you fool, for thirteen years you've believed.

JUDITH: Yes, I believe!

AMELIA: He said to me, thirteen years ago he said, "Amelia, I'm broke…just a little loan to tide me over, but don't tell her, for God's sake don't tell her."

JUDITH: You're lying!

AMELIA: Not *now*… Do you think this is easy for me…Daisy out there, just as you were once. My little suckling, my little babe.

JUDITH: And now?

AMELIA: And now I realize that for this entire fiscal year I have totally supported you while you ignore the whole problem. Judith, while you give parties that are reported in the society pages I am selling my stocks. The country is booming with the war. An all time high…but Arthur is at an all time low.

JUDITH: He did say something—just last week he said, "We're a little short this month, Judy."

AMELIA: And what did you do about it?

JUDITH: I cancelled the Limoges I ordered.

AMELIA: Five hundred Detroit Edison, three hundred American Tel and Tel.

JUDITH: Amelia…if he *was* short, and he did say he was—you know how expensive the repairs are on the cottage on Monhegan, a new roof, reshingling, the flag pole falling through the windows in the living room.

AMELIA: Sold, you fool! Ace sold the cottage. Sold it six months ago!

JUDITH: Never! He couldn't. It's…it's mine…daddy's, your's… Never, never.

AMELIA: Ask him yourself. I only see him with bills in his hand, saying, "Don't tell her, please, don't tell her.

JUDITH: The cottage? The cottage gone? He would have *told* me!

AMELIA: You only see him with a glass in his hand, toasting a contract he never got!

JUDITH: You've changed, Amelia, changed—you used to be gentle.

AMELIA: I never changed one iota!

JUDITH: Something *happened* to you!

AMELIA: Thirteen years happened to me; this house happened to me; Daisy happened to me.

JUDITH: Daisy is part yours, Daisy out there singing her little song.

AMELIA: She'll smell of money shortly.

JUDITH: You're hard, Amelia, you're.like a man.

AMELIA: Hard am I! Ask him ·then.

JUDITH: You're sick! You speak with a double heart. A heart that opens once for Daisy and once for your change purse.

AMELIA: Don't rebuke me. See if he's man enough to tell you.

JUDITH: You'd better take a pill. You act like a man, a two fisted man!

(AMY *crosses center, then to* DAISY; JUDITH *sits stool.*)

DAISY: HEY, DADDY. I WANT A BRAND NEW CAR, CHAMPAGNE, CAVIAR…HEY, DADDY…

AMELIA: Here! It's a five dollar bill. *(She tears up bill.)* Now how do you like that! That's what your mother does. She's not real, that powder puff Judith. And as for your father, that drunkard. We never had a drunkard, or a divorce or a democrat in our family.

DAISY: Mother voted for Roosevelt.

AMELIA: Would you like a ten? You could tear it up all by yourself!

DAISY: Aunt Amy! It's me. It's Daisy.

AMELIA: Never mind who it is! I wasn't always an accountant. I had to throw away the violets he gave me. I had to be a lady—a lady all my life.

DAISY: You don't have to be an accountant. Daddy can hire one.

AMELIA: You're altogether filthy and will eat of my money. (*She crosses right to prie-dieu.*)

(DAISY *crosses to* JUDITH.)

DAISY: Mother? What's wrong with me? Oh, mother!

JUDITH: I'll be eaten up by all of you, piece by piece. Another person coming in here with questions, with "me, me, me" in their eyes.

DAISY: I'm all mixed up.

JUDITH: Yes, of course. Corne here, dear. Sit down beside me Daisy, stay the same. Daisy mine, you're the pure one in this house. You're the small one of the big ones.

DAISY: Aunt Amy doesn't love me any more. She called me dirty and she tore up a five dollar bill.

JUDITH: She's turning sour.

DAISY: She doesn't talk the same. Why does she think she's an accountant?

JUDITH: It's nerves. The doctor has put her on phenobarbital for her nerves.

DAISY: I'm afraid.

JUDITH: And just last night telling the cook that the tomato bisque was poisoned.

DAISY: Around ten she cried in her room. But when I went in she hugged me and we had a back rub and it was all over then.

JUDITH: One minute hugging you, next minute hard and cruel with me. Always when I've thought of the word backbone I've thought of Aunt Amy. My mother and Aunt Amy were born sitting up straight. I see them in corsets and high collars, but when I see myself I'm in a speakeasy. You'd never have been born if it hadn't been for bathtub gin. Don't touch me!

DAISY: I didn't mean to.

JUDITH: Of course, dear.

DAISY: Are you worried about Aunt Amy?

JUDITH: Both your father and Aunt Amy...Doctor Barstow said he is a confirmed alcoholic.

AMELIA: *(AMY down center)* I am the tongue of the shoe. Let me touch the tongue of Daisy with its curses and deceits and frauds.

DAISY: I hate growing up and learning those things.

AMELIA: I eat the dust from the dustbin.

DAISY: It scares me.

JUDITH: Don't be scared. It's perfectly safe. It always will be.

AMELIA: I am not a checkbook, I am a woman.

JUDITH: As long as you stay my little girl.

DAISY: That's what Aunt Amy says after we hug and kiss.

AMELIA: The bull has conquered me.

JUDITH: It makes me shiver the way Aunt Amy keeps stroking you.

DAISY: What's wrong with touching people?

AMELIA: My bones are immense.

JUDITH: Women don't touch women that way.

AMELIA: I am a flagpole of bones.

DAISY: She's my best friend.

AMELIA: My bowels swell and fill my garments.

JUDITH: You go to bed now. Read or something.

AMELIA: I have burst from my mother's thighs and breasts.

DAISY: Are you and daddy all right?

JUDITH: We have things to discuss tonight.

(DAISY *crosses right to right platform and takes teddy.*)

AMELIA: *(At prie-dieu)* Some trust in chariots and some in Lincoln Continentals.

(ARTHUR *enters upstage left with Scotch bottle; crosses toward* JUDITH.)

JUDITH: Ace?

ARTHUR: Yes?

JUDITH: Aren't you coming to bed?

ARTHUR: It's only a nightcap.

JUDITH: A bottle in the bedroom!

AMELIA: I swallow down my spittle. I have sinned.

ARTHUR: So?

JUDITH: Ace!

AMELIA: Am I sea, or a whale or a bonefish, that thou settest a watch over me?

JUDITH: Ace, stop it. What's going on?

ARTHUR: All I got's my bottle. Remember that, Judy, remember that. All I got's my bottle. I'm all cleaned out now! Himself 's been cleaned out of nickles. Himself's been cleaned out of dimes.

AMELIA: My flesh is clothed in worms and clumps of dust. My skin is broken with pus and I shall lie down with a leper.

JUDITH: Spin Ryan at Boothbay Harbor, all that summer… "Been cleaned out of nickles, been cleaned out of dimes!" He said it every time you won a jackpot.

AMELIA: I am strangling on my soul. It is stuck like a sock in my mouth. There is a spider web in my sinus, growing out of my nose.

ARTHUR: Remember that first day? I'd just won the race at the Yacht Club and we walked over to Spin Ryan's store and that artist fellow was playing the nickle machine and I touched up the ten center and after six tries.

JUDITH: The three bars jackpot!

AMELIA: The Lord is a liemaker. He is a physician of no value.

ARTHUR: Down she vomited, all cleaned out—two quarts of dimes and fourteen more dollars.

JUDITH: And Spin Ryan stood there all red nosed clutching his bottle of rye.

ARTHUR: Saying "That machine ain't spewed in a month".

JUDITH: The dimes ran all over the floor!

AMELIA: Woman that is born of woman is of few days.

ARTHUR: And I paid your father's store bill and had a pocketful left.

JUDITH: And you said I had to marry you, that brought you luck.

ARTHUR: And that we'd live off Spin Ryan's machine.

AMELIA: I came forth like poison ivy, a flower to be cut down. I die and waste away for I can bring forth no child, nor tend no sheep, nor plant no olive trees.

JUDITH: Oh, Ace, you're such a winner. Aunt Amy lied, You didn't s sell the cottage did you? The cottage at Monhegan, daddy's house. She said it was sold.

AMELIA: And the mountain has leaned on me all day and the Lord has pierced me with picks and my mouth closest on tacks.

ARTHUR: I sold it—she's right.

JUDITH: That isn't all she said.

ARTHUR: I suppose she said I was broke!

JUDITH: That's what she *said*.

ARTHUR: It's true, all of its true. I'm broke, I'm a loser now, Judy, a loser.

AMELIA: Not one of you can bring a clean thing out of an unclean thing. When you fill your belly it will fill only with bowel movement. There is no hope for what passest through.

JUDITH: You bastard. You sold the cottage! Don't give me that loser talk.

ARTHUR: It's Amelia's fault. She said, when I married you she said—

JUDITH: You were the best salesman in the country—

AMELIA: Oh, father, father, why do you whip me?

ARTHUR: I was—once I was. Honest to God, Judy, I didn't want to sell the cottage.

AMELIA: Whip me will you, father! Here take this.

Yes, father I know. In our house we follow the teaching of Christ!

JUDITH: It's gone. Never mind. It' s gone… And you took from Aunt Amy. All these years you took from her. You were a weak man—

ARTHUR: Weak hell!

AMELIA: Goodnight, father, goodnight.

ARTHUR: My luck ran out. Judy, that machine ain't spewed in years.

AMELIA: No, of course, we didn't go to church. Not we. Yes, father, you you had a disagreement with it.

JUDITH: What's that mean now?

AMELIA: You brought home those marble statues from Rome. You put one in the foyer with water spouting from its little mouth.

ARTHUR: I mean I need a drink… Here have a swig.

JUDITH: I don't drink straight from the bottle!

AMELIA: And when the preacher came to call he said that you could not have nude statues in your house. He told you it was pagan, father!

ARTHUR: All I got' s my bottle.

AMELIA: So you never went to church again. Whip me will you, father?

JUDITH: This isn't a bedroom any more. It's a barroom.

AMELIA: So, every Sunday we all gathered in the drawing room while you read the Bible aloud for two hours.

JUDITH: Why didn't you tell me about the cottage yourself?

AMELIA: Two long hours, father!

ARTHUR: I didn't want to look at your face when I told you.

AMELIA: All eight of us sat in a row with our hands folded and never moved a muscle.

JUDITH: You never look at me anymore, anyhow.

ARTHUR: More than you think!

AMELIA: Father, then one Sunday in June I fell asleep. I dozed off.

JUDITH: You spend all your time looking in a Scotch glass.

AMELIA: And you whipped me with your riding crop.

ARTHUR: Forgive me, Judy. I lied...I lied.

AMELIA: Oh, father, father, let all mine enemies be ashamed and whipped.

JUDITH: You took money from Amelia. You cheat... You thief.

ARTHUR: Okay, I groveled in front of Amelia... Is that what you want of me?

JUDITH: I can't stand you this way. You disgust me!

AMELIA: Open my legs and fill me with tears and chasten me with thy hot displeasure.

ARTHUR: Judy!

JUDITH: Get out of here for good. Get going!

AMELIA: God, goodnight, father.

ARTHUR: Lock the door, will you? Okay, lock it up tight, Judith, and dream your little locked up dreams...

DAISY: (*Sitting platform right*) I think words are stupid, don't you, teddy. I bet if you could talk you'd say the same thing. Everyone talks to themselves anyhow... No one really listens...except you, teddy... *You* know just what I mean.

JUDITH: Sleep in the guest room, Ace, and take your bottle to bed with you!

DAISY: Oh Teddy, I·wish they'd stop. I wish.Aunt Amy would come in and cuddle me.

ARTHUR: Why do you shut me out? Why now? When I need you.

AMELIA: I had to throw away the violets he gave me. They floated right down the canal. Even in Venice I'm a lady. I cannot see him any longer. Cannot, cannot. Must not listen any longer to his words of love when I know he is married. Cannot. Cannot. I must be a lady; a lady all my life.

(JUDITH *out left*)

ARTHUR: No more from her, that princess girl. Not another word. *(Left of center)* The moon is red-faced tonight… Oh, God, I wonder what a red-faced moon means? …What would the fisherman say tonight about her—her eyes bulging *(To* DAISY*)* Asleep, Daisy?

DAISY: No, daddy, not quite.

ARTHUR: Would you like to cuddle?

DAISY: Cuddle?

ARTHUR: *(Bottle in hand)* Hell, Daisy, I'm lonely.

DAISY: I know.

ARTHUR: No good anymore, Daisy-bell, no good daddy anymore. But when I'm drunk I forget about that. When I drink I feel pretty damn good again.

DAISY: I love you and you're not no good, even if you are always drinking.

AMELIA: Tonight is the night of the night watches.

ARTHUR: You too! What the hell. I have no home at all around here.

AMELIA: Touch my skin, oh, Lord, according to your maps and Baedeckers.

ARTHUR: Just because I drink a little my house is being eaten up on me in a million chunks by a hungry rat.

AMELIA: According to the tribe of Loveworthy, my feet shall be washed in brine and I shall neither slumber nor sleep.

DAISY: Oh, no, daddy! I didn't mean *that*. I mean I love you anyhow!

ARTHUR: My Daisy, my Daisy-bell.

DAISY: Sing me the song.

ARTHUR: That's right. I'd forgotten that song. I'd forgotten I was the one who named you Daisy. The summer you learned to walk. I'd throw you up·in the air like a toy and sing it. Though Amelia, that haughty bitch, never forgave us for calling you that. Daisy-bell, first flower of my heart.

AMELIA: I shall keep vigil with my clock on the right hand and my enema bag on the left.

ARTHUR: Someday we'll get the bike built for two.

AMELIA & ARTHUR: *(Sing together)* There is a flower in hy heart, Daisy, Daisy! Planted one day by a glancing dart planted by Daisy-bell! Whether she loves me or loves me not. Sometimes it's hard to tell: yet I am longing to share the lot of beau-ti-ful Daisy-bell! Dai-sy, Dai-sy give me your answer do! —I'm half crazy, all for the love of you! It won't be a stylish marriage, I can't afford a carriage, but you'll look sweet upon the seat of a bicycle built for two.

DAISY: Oh, daddy, you're the most fun of all.

AMELIA: My teeth are in place and my tongue, that little bird, flutters in its cage.

ARTHUR: It leaves you thirsty.

AMELIA: I am fighting with my groaning all night. All night I am swimming in oil and it clouds my eyes.

ARTHUR: Well, Daisy-bell-girl not a little girl anymore, a grown woman.

DAISY: I'm cold out here. Guess I'll get under the covers. *(Lies down)*

ARTHUR: Fine. Let me stretch out, too. *(Lies down)* What's this?

DAISY: Teddy.

ARTHUR: Pretty silly for a grown woman to take a stuffed animal to bed with her. Me! I can't even take a woman to bed.

AMELIA: I will keep blessed my breasts. They will rest on my ribs like two sleeping swans.

ARTHUR: When you drink all day no one wants you, if you do get a woman to bed, it doesn't work—you lose your erection.

DAISY: What's an erection?

ARTHUR: Nothing…just something men get when they get to be men.

DAISY: Do girls get it, too?

ARTHUR: Nope . Doesn't work that way. Here, we'll make a woman of you yet. Take some. No. Three swallows.

DAISY: I don't like it.

ARTHUR: A few swallows. You ·will. It's good for you, prewar Scotch, like medicine.

AMELIA: *(During speech,* DAISY *takes three swallows.)* Once I was a shedder of blood and the great eagle took me in his claws and came into my mouth and ate thereof. He traded me for figs and oil and wine. He drank of me and caused me shame.

DAISY: It burns like fire.

ARTHUR: Now you're really grown up, had your first drink with your old man, got the—menstruated last month.

DAISY: How did you know?

ARTHUR: Your mother said.

DAISY: Do you know if it only happens once a year?

AMELIA: The days of the month are sacred, and I will wash them.

ARTHUR: No, once a month if you're lucky.

DAISY: Lucky?

ARTHUR: Just a joke of your mother's. Lie down now and I'll give you a back rub the way Aunt Amy does. You have breasts, too, don't you. Nice little peachy breasts. Does it feel good?

AMELIA: I am clean. I am sweeter than honeycomb and the bees buzz over my mouth.

ARTHUR: Oh, Daisy, I'm so lonely. I need someone to love me.

AMELIA: I will stroke my skin with cream and let the virgins admire me. I will build my womb like the ribs of a dory and when my little girl comes to me I will let her lie betwixt my breasts.

ARTHUR: Daisy, lie close to me.

DAISY: Yes, daddy, yes.

AMELIA: (Crosses down left and discovers them) Were you calling, Daisy? I thought I heard a voice—Arthur!

ARTHUR: Amelia, I—

AMELIA: Disgusting!

DAISY: Why do you cry, daddy?

AMELIA: Filthy…both of you!

DAISY: Only fire water, Aunt Amy—only—

AMELIA: And drinking, too…oh, the filth of it, the horrible filth of it!

ARTHUR: Go to sleep, little flower girl. *(Out up left)*

AMELIA: And a seed shall serve him and it shall be accounted to the Lord for a generation.

DAISY: I want my teddy bear.

AMELIA: Take your filthy teddy bear!

(AMELIA kicks teddy to her: DAISY sits.)

DAISY: Oh, teddy, what happened to you?

(Tape: choir singing Sanctus)

PRIEST: *(Enters up right, crossees and exits audience right)* Why died I not from the womb? Why did I not give up the ghost when I came out of the belly? Why did the knees prevent me? Or the breasts that I should suck?

(PRIEST on tape, over:)

PRIEST: For now·I should have lain still and been quiet, I should have slept: then had I been at rest.

AMELIA: A doctor, Judith says! A little rest for Amelia! And Daisy's still asleep! And Arthur asleep and Judith will tell the cook—that heathen cook—that I'm indisposed— Indisposed!! Poor Judith… Oh, it's too comical, too ludicrous… *(Crosses up right to throne)* Who put the hex into Texas! Ha! And they put you away for knowing that! Oh, I keep doubling off. It's like purling off…no…it's like casting off. You make a double, a conversation that goes on between your two selves and then it starts … starts to scream obscene things and then it rolls down the hill and the other joins in, howling with laughter, calling off its own words, own signals, little plaything, away from itself… then these two are over, are dead… They are cast off, double trouble.

DAISY: *(Crosses to* AMY *on throne)* Aunt Amy, I feel sick.

AMELIA: Who are you? I don't know you.

DAISY: I'm Daisy...Aunt Amy, what's wrong?

AMELIA: No, you're not. You can't fool me that easily, bringing a fradulent Daisy in here to trap me.

DAISY: Oh, please...don't play games.

AMELIA: Go burn in hell where you belong.

DAISY: Oh, poor Aunt Amy, what do you mean? Why do you cry?

AMELIA: *(Like a child)* I heard ghosts again, all night. That terrible ghost came in beating the bedstead like a drummer. Then I couldn't move. He was wrapping chains around my arms and legs.

DAISY: You had a nightmare.

AMELIA: I was weighted down and I called out for my mama to help me but she didn't hear. And then the ghost was panting and scratching for half an hour beside my dressing table, and I didn't dare speak out... Next he was in the maid's room, knocking about for a while.

DAISY: I'm here, Aunt Amy...Daisy's here. There isn't any ghost here. No one will hurt you.

AMELIA: Oh, get away from me, have you no pity. I keep doubling off. *(Crosses and sits right bench)*

*(*CHOIR *sings* Gradual *as* PRIEST *on tape:)*

PRIEST: Beware of false prophets, which come to you in sheep's clothing, but inwardly they are ravening wolves. Ye shall know them by their fruit. Do men gather grapes of	DAISY: Don't you. love me anymore?
	AMELIA: I love *Daisy.*
	DAISY: If I'm not Daisy,

thorns, or figs of of thistles?
Even so every good tree
bringeth forth good fruit;
but a corrupt ·tree bringeth
forth evil fruit. A good tree
cannot bring forth evil fruit,
neither can a corrupt tree
bring forth good fruit. Every
tree that bringeth not forth
good fruit is hewn down,
and cast into the fire. Not
everyone that saith unto
me Lord, Lord, shall enter
into the kingdom of
Heaven.

then who am I?

(PRIEST *enters audience
right, crosses to stage
center.)*

DR ALEX: Come Daisy's
Aunt. You're crazy now.
You're being put away
and you'll never get out.

AMELIA: Give me my hat!
I want the hat with the
strawberries on it. I
refuse to go without a
hat! A lady always wears
a hat. Unclean! No Daisy
ever!

(AMELIA *exits with* PRIEST.)

(ARTHUR *enters up left and crosses to center.* DAISY *crosses
to center and meets* ARTHUR.)

ARTHUR: Where is she? Daisy, Daisy, birthday girl. All
grown up now aren't you birthday Daisy. A fine young
husband and now a baby.· Twenty-seven, is that right?

DAISY: That's right, Daddy. Twenty-seven.

ARTHUR: What's that?

DAISY: It's Abigail. She's crying. Can I go up and see
what's wrong?

ARTHUR: All right, but don't tell your mother.

DAISY: I'm well enough to be home for the weekend.

ARTHUR: Just take a little look.

DAISY: Can't I hold her? She's my baby.

ARTHUR: Oh, Daisy, you *know.*

DAISY: Yes. I know.

ARTHUR: Hurry, before your mother comes back. *(Out up left.)*

(DAISY crosses to right platform.)

DAISY: Is she alive? Oh, don't let her die all alone. Oh, Daisy, shut up! She's not going to die. I don't even know any lullabies...or any prayers either. *(Sings softly)* Baby, baby, give me your answer true. I'm half crazy over the love of you. I'm half crazy. *(Stops singing)* Mummy's here. But you don't know who Mummy is, do you? How could you? Not so close or she'll breathe me in and die of it.

(JUDITH enters right.)

JUDITH: What are you doing up here? Is anything wrong with my baby? She's sound asleep and you'll just disturb her.

DAISY: I'll never get her back; back in my contagious arms.

JUDITH: Come down and be a good birthday girl.

DAISY: She was coughing. There was a wishbone caught in her throat. That sound, like a dog choking.

JUDITH: Oh, stop it! You were always this way...if someone crossed the street then they were dead. You act just like Aunt Amy when...when she had her upset. Now stop this nonsense and come right down...Daisy, come. Fear is not good, fear can be catching. *(Out right)*

CHOIR: *(Tape)* And I look for the resurrection of the dead and the life of the world to come.

DAISY: O Mary, fragile mother, hear me, hear me now. I am the unbeliever. O Mary, permit me this grace, this crossing over. Word for word I stumble. A beginner, I feel your mouth touch mine. Closer and closer comes

the hour of my death as I rearrange my face, grow
back, grow undeveloped and straight haired. I lie like
a dog on the carpet. In the mind there is a thin alley
called death and I move through it as through water.
Now I have entered the year without words. I note
the queer entrance and the exact voltage. Without
words one may touch bread and be handed bread
and make no sound. O Mary, tender physician, come
with powders and herbs. For I am in the center. It is
very small and the air is gray as in a steam house. I am
handed wine as a child is handed milk. It is presented
in a delicate glass with a round bowl and a thin lip.
The wine itself is pitch colored, musty and secret. The
glass rises on its own toward my mouth. The glass tilts
in on its own and I am on fire. I see two thin streaks
burn down my chin. I have been cut in two. O Mary,
open your eyelids. I am in the domain of silence, the
kingdom of the crazy and the sleeper. There is blood
here and I have eaten it. O mother of the womb, did I
come for blood alone?

DR ALEX: *(Enters right)* Daisy.

DAISY: O little mother, I am in my own mind. Wrong
house. I am locked in the wrong house.

DR ALEX: Daisy, you're not alone. I'm here too.

DAISY: My Aunt Amy. I don't know anyone but her.

DR ALEX: Daisy come back then we'll have a cigarette
and a drink together. Things of this world, not things
of the dead. Together, not alone. I'm not Aunt Amy. I
smoke. I drink. I'm here. I will not become Aunt Amy.

DAISY: Don't lie to me, you're my Aunt Amy.

DR ALEX: Stop kidding yourself. Not everyone who is
nice to you is your Aunt Amy. You know who I am.
I'm Doctor Alex, your Doctor Alex.

DAISY: I think my Aunt Amy was taken away by a doctor.

DR ALEX: I had nothing to do with her. Some doctor took her away at one time because she was crazy and you thought you were responsible for it.

DAISY: Bring her back.

DR ALEX: I can't.

DAISY: Can. Oh Aunt Amy I have the magic.

DR ALEX: No you don't have magic like that. No one does. Do you want to live with this all your life? A woman who keeps hoarding sleeping pills. A haunted little girl who sees Christ in frying pans. Who's afraid to go to the super market, who had to leave Europe because of a ghost who followed her from cafe to cafe in Venice. A little girl who can't do anything because she's afraid.

DAISY: I'm not afraid, I have my Aunt Amy.

DR ALEX: If you want to be alone inside your own world you can be; if you want help you can have it. Which will it be?

DAISY: I love Aunt Amy enough for everyone.

DR ALEX: And what about me?

DAISY: Aunt Amy.

DR ALEX: Now damn it to Hell you recognize me, I'm here, I'm real, I had onion for lunch, smell them; that's alive. Skin. Nerves. Pores on the face! Aunt Amy is rotten by now. No skin. No tendons. No breath. No eyes. Disintegrated. Part of the casket that's part of the earth.

DAISY: You can not change the night into day.

DR ALEX: Daisy, which is it you want?

DAISY: I have made my bed in the fire and Aunt Amy
will speak of the fire and of the beasts and you will be
vile in her sight and afterward we will speak.

DR ALEX: Things of ·this world or things of the dead.
(Exits right.)

(AMELIA enters right.)

DAISY: The grave is my house.

AMELIA: Daisy, this is my hand. My hand in your hand.
You're grown up now. All that was a long time ago.
Now tell me, who am I?

DAISY: Aunt Amy, I prayed for you and now you're
here.

AMELIA: I'm here. I always will be.

DAISY: Aunt Amy, don't lie to me.

AMELIA: I'm not.

DAISY: You died in the fire. The roof, the house. All of
you burned up in the house. Mother, Daddy.

AMELIA: We didn't burn. We all died in bed. When
you were three the hotel on Monhegan burned.
Everyone on the south side of the island got into boats.
I wrapped you in a blanket and put you in your brmvn
wicker stroller. The whole island got up that night. We
were worried the whole island would go, as quick as a
pine fire.

DAISY: All I can remember is gripping onto my stroller.

AMELIA: You were safe. You were with me.

DAISY: I prayed for you. For years I prayed for you.

AMELIA: We've prayed together many times, you and I.

DAISY: But when I pray, I pray about the fire. My fire.

AMELIA: Right now I don't recommend prayer. Right
now I recommend cocoa and saltines.

DAISY: Don't leave me, for God's sake, don't leave me!

AMELIA: O, little namesake, surely I know what's best for you.

DAISY: But Christ. I need him to forgive me for the fire.

AMELIA: Nonsense! Cocoa and saltines. *(Out up right)*

DAISY: *(Follows to prie-dieu; picks up ceborium top)* Things of this world. Will they do it for me? Fire and desire, they will kill. Twelve years of being mentally ill. I'm not ill, I'm diseased. It's not my mind that's diseased, it's my soul. Surely, Doctor Alex would say, surely things are better with your family? Yes, he's right…and yet…and yet? If it is better, then why am I shrinking this way? While women dream of their manicures and permanents, I lie down at night with my head on the pillow and hear rats eating under the lawns, breeding in the cesspools and the sewers. I'm tired of trying to be a woman, tired of the spoons, and the pots, tired of my mouth and my breasts, tired of the cosmetics and the silk dresses. I'm even tired of my father with his white bone…I'm tired of the gender of things. Last night I had a dream and when I woke up I said "You are the answer. You will outlive my husband and my father" …In that dream there was a city made of chains where Joan was put to death in man's clothes and the nature of the angels went unexplained, no two made in the same species. One had an ear in its hand! One was chewing a star and recording its orbit! They were all obeying themselves, performing God's functions. A people apart. "You are the answer," I said to them and then I entered, lying down on the gates of their city. Then chains were fastened around me and I lost my gender, my womanhood. Adam was on the left of me and Eve was on the right of me…both thoroughly inconsistent with the world of the reason. We wove our arms together and rode under a kind of sun. I

was not a woman anymore! Not one thing or other. O
daughters of Jerusalem, the king has brought me into
his chamber…I am black and I am beautiful. I've been
opened and undressed. I have no arms or legs. I'm all
one skin like a fish. I'm no more a woman…than Christ
was a man. Oh, Daisy, a dream is not a vision of God. I
don't have any prayers, any real prayers. All I have is a
need, a dream. Oh Jesus, look down from your tree of
nails, your never-moving tree of nails and tell me. Take
me out of my body and give me back my soul. I didn't
say I was a saint. You've come back! You're moving!
You're breathing! You're calling my name! Your
fingers are thin as pencils and your mouth, Christ,
open like the sore of a fish where it's been hooked…
Your hands… Oh my God, your hands… Your hands
with great holes in them and the blood is all sticky and
brown and red…and…oh Christ, I'm calling to you
because of the fire, because of everyone that day of the
fire…watched the house burn—red, red…someone was
whipping a horse on the lawn, but I didn't move …
watched them burn down inside it. They were burned
up like roast pigs on a spit. I let it happen!!! Oh Christ,
will no one forgive me for it? Can I undo a fire, Christ,
with a wound? Christ, busy with your own dying,
don't leave me behind. Wait for me. Wait for me and
forgive me. Blood, like a handful of drinking water!
Dear Christ! Thank you.

DR ALEX: *(Enters down center)* Daisy, what's happened
to your hand. You're hurt!

DAISY: It's real. Don't you see it?

DR ALEX Of course I see it, but what happened?

DAISY: It's the…the stigmata!

DR ALEX: The *what*?

DAISY: The stigmata of Christ!

DR ALEX: Don't be a fool, Daisy. You're getting blood on my new carpet. How did you cut it?

DAISY: I was here alone waiting for you and it happened—Christ came back to me and—I told him about the fire and then He came back.

DR ALEX: But the cut?

DAISY: Oh that...that! That happened before today too.

DR ALEX: You cut yourself before—

DAISY: Yes, yes!

DR ALEX: You've never mentioned it.

DAISY: You wouldn't have liked it... You would have laughed.

DR ALEX: Daisy, what is it that you want me to *do*?

DAISY: To believe!

DR ALEX: Now I see. That's just what it is you do want... Now... Begin with the first cut—the first—stigmata you had.

DAISY: I went down into the subway to come in here. I had to go to the "john" and I couldn't find my way to the ladies' room and I started to cry and this deformed man came up to me and said, "Hey, lady! You okay? You got bloody hands. Want me to call the cops?"

DR ALEX: On the subway, all by yourself...with Christ...

DAISY: And I ran away from him, shoving my hands into my pockets to protect them. I had gloves on—they were all wet and red.

DR ALEX: Gloves?

DAISY: I threw them away in the ladies' room. They were all bloody. When I got in there I saw two women standing and talking over the washbowls putting on lipstick so I went into the "john" and took off the gloves. Blood all over them.

DR ALEX: Oh God, I just don't know about you. Stigmata with gloves on. Always the lady, always the sinner…

DAISY: I was afraid to let anyone see that, so I kneeled down on the floor and flushed the toilet and washed them off, over and over in the toilet bowl.

DR ALEX: And when did you decide that it was Christ's blood, not yours?

DAISY: In the "john"!

DR ALEX: If I were Christ I wouldn't want to be found in a "john".

DAISY: He doesn't mind at all!

DR ALEX: Daisy, come off it! Perhaps you ought to be talking to a priest.

DAISY: I saw one

DR ALEX: Today?

DAISY: After the subway—before you.

DR ALEX: Did he help at all?

DAISY: He offered me brandy, he had half his altar boys down with measles, and a curate with the flu. All he did was drink brandy and tell me to return to the sacraments.

DR ALEX: Not what you wanted?

DAISY: I wanted Christ…only Christ.

DR ALEX: Daisy, don't shut me out again. There's a reason for everything, even Christ, even death.

DAISY: Even my sickness! That silly thing! I've left it all behind—cut it out of me.

DR ALEX: As you cut yourself for Christ?

DAISY: A gift of blood, He said, was for hire...redder than death, truer than fire. The fire was for me but the blood is for Him.

DR ALEX: Does it hurt?

DAISY: A lie would hurt less...God bless lies.

DR ALEX: Well, there's one lie He won't bless today. It's about time you recognized this! Do you remember now? Remember stabbing yourself with it?

DAISY: What does it mean?

DR ALEX: You did it yourself, stabbed yourself, gave yourself your own stigmata!

DAISY: Oh God, God damn it!

DR ALEX: It's all right, Daisy, I knew it anyhow. Only *you* had to face it.

DAISY: Then none of it was true?

DR ALEX: None.

DAISY: I'm such a fool. Poor little wound. It didn't even hurt much.

DR ALEX: You wanted it to hurt more?

DAISY: Yes more.

DR ALEX: Daisy, you want to be hurt because you are afraid of the past, afraid of the dead. Because you refuse to face anything.

DAISY: Dead is red and dead and red have gone have gone to bed, she said.

DR ALEX: Daisy, are you hoarding sleeping pills again?

DAISY: Of course, Doc, bottles and bottles of them over the stove beside the basil and the thyme.

DR ALEX: You want to be dead, too.

DAISY: Yes...death is a sleep, a sleep I could keep.

DR ALEX: Death? Even if there is no Christ?

DAISY: Don't talk that way, Doctor Alex, talk language. It's a way to talking that talks.

DR ALEX: I'm not afraid of your language.

DAISY: When I was ten, our dog Pickle, his eyes were full of brown language.

DR ALEX: Are you sure his name was Pickle?

DAISY: I don't mean Pickle. What do I mean? I mean pickle-dickle-dickery-dock, the mouse ran up the clock, the clock ran down, his name was blue, his name was brown… That's it! Brownie was his name…I forgot that.

DR ALEX: Brownie's eyes were full of language?

DAISY: Yes.

DR ALEX: Language is okay with me too—after all, that's how we communicate.

DAISY: Language has nothing to do with rational things. Language is the opposite of the way a machine works.

DR ALEX: There are no machines in here.

DAISY: Just dreams… Do dreams go into machines? Does breath go into death? …My friend, Death…

DR ALEX: Thinking about death again?

DAISY: Yes… Yes, I am.

DR ALEX: I think you'd better go into the hospital for a few days. I can't let you go off into the night half cocked like this, stabbing things into your hands, rhyming onto the street.

DAISY: Hospital?

DR ALEX: Yes. You've been there before.

DAISY: I knew when I came in; I came prepared.

DR ALEX: All right then…

DR ALEX: *(V O)* …Doctor Alex here. I have a patient for admission. Mrs Robert Cullen for emergency psychiatric. Send an ambulance over here, nine-oh-nine Beacon Street. I will medicate Mrs Cullen…I'll see her in the morning… Thank you.

DAISY: *(During the above)* Whom are you calling while I am falling?

DR ALEX: The hospital where you'll go tonight. And now I'll give you a little injection that will help you sleep.

DAISY: Needles frighten me!

DR ALEX: It's only a little Thorazine to help you sleep.

DAISY: Needles mean fear is near. But it didn't hurt… will it give me a sleep I can keep?

DR ALEX: For a while. Yes, Daisy, you can keep your sleep for a while.

DAISY: It will be scarey to be dead, going alone like a child afraid, walking down the dark cellar stairs into God knows what!

DR ALEX: There is no cellar, no blood, no Christ like yours. Listen to me, Daisy, you're not alone.

DAISY: Am I going away like Aunt Amy, all crazy?

DR ALEX: You're not Aunt Amy at all.

DAISY: Love is a glove and the glove is all red.

DR ALEX: There was no real glove, only a real love. Languarge. Language again.

DAISY: Words aren't much good, are they?

DR ALEX: All we have.

DAISY: Oh, I feel so dirty.

DR ALEX: What rhymes with dirty?

DAISY: I'm tired of what rhymes.

DR ALEX: Sure?

DAISY: It's all a riddle in the end... And if I die, where will I lie? And if I leave me, where will I grieve me? ...I'll do it right, my leaving and grieving...

DR ALEX: You're a funny girl, Daisy. I think I'll call you Mrs Language.

DAISY: Lazy, hazy, crazy Daisy. Doctor Alex, do you remember when you took me as a patient?

DR ALEX: Yes, I remember. I remember, too, how far you've come.

DAISY: I mean when you said to me, "I have room," and then I knew that someone else spoke language. It meant you weren't afraid. Having room is the opposite of being in the closet.

DR ALEX: You mean when you were a child and hid in the closet?

DAISY: That's what I mean. "I have room," you said. I want to thank you for all you've done. It sounds silly, but I want to thank you—no matter what happens to me, I still thank you. "I have room." No one ever said that to me except Aunt Amy.

DR ALEX: You were lonely. I'll see you tomorrow.

DAISY: Tomorrow is full of sorrow...oh dog, oh dog! Here I go...just like Aunt Amy.

DR ALEX: No. Daisy... Meanwhile you can sleep.

DAISY: Oh, little sleep...a sleep I can keep.

(DR ALEX *out up left*.)

(DAISY *kneels at altar*; ACOLYTES *enter*.)

PRIEST: (*V O*) Almighty God, our heavenly Father, who of His great mercy hath promised forgiveness of sins to all those who with hearty repentance and true faith turn unto him, have mercy upon you, pardon and deliver you from all your sins.

DAISY: *(Crosses to right platform)* If I'm not Daisy then who am I?

ACOLYTES: The Bible, the Bible, get Daisy to bring the Bible, the corset, the little Italian clock, and the enema bag.

DAISY: Fear is not good. Fear can be catching.

DR ALEX: *(Enters left to pulpit)* Daisy, are you hoarding sleeping pills again?

DAISY: Oh, teddy, what's happened to you?

DR ALEX: That's all the fire. That's all the desire. Come home now.

ACOLYTES: I'm the king of the castle and you're the dirty rascal. The strawberries, the strawberries, the corset, the corset, the little Italian clock, the little Italian clock, the enema bag, the enema hag, the Bible, the Bible, the sleeping pills, the sleeping pills.

DAISY: The Bible… That's where Christ lives! Give me my Christ!

DR ALEX: Don't hide from me. I'm here. I'm real!

DAISY: I think I hear Christ calling to me.

DR ALEX: It's me, Daisy. It's me. Come back to me.

DAISY: Now, now, Daisy. You're imagining things. I'm quite tired of imagining things. I think I'll just go to sleep.

DR ALEX: You're not Aunt Amy at all.

DAISY: Not Abigail! Dear God, not Abigail too!

DR ALEX: God damn you, Daisy. Get back here where you belong.

DAISY: But Abigail is only thirteen years old!

ACOLYTES: I'm the king of the castle and you're a dirty rascal. The strawberries, the strawberries, the corset, the corset, the little Italian clock, the little Italian clock, the enema bag, the enema bag, the Bible, the Bible, the sleeping pills, the sleeping pills.

DR ALEX: You hear me. I know you hear me. Daisy. Please. Please!

DAISY: I'm locked in the wrong house. I can't get out. I can't get out.

DR ALEX: Daisy, you have been brought forth from a stiff-necked people. Daisy, the zeal of your house doth eat you up. O Daisy, O Daughter of Jerusalem, there is an enormous hunger in Zion.

(Sound: Choir singing Agnus Dei*)*

PRIEST: *(V O)* Grant us therefore, gracious Lord, so to eat the flesh of thy dear Son Jesus Christ, and to drink his blood, that our sinful bodies may be made clean by His body and our souls washed through His most precious blood. Behold the lamb of God who takes away the sins of the world.

PRIEST: Daisy, the body of Christ. *(He gives her the wafer.)* Daisy, the blood of Christ. *(Gives her the drink from the chalice.)*

(Sound: Choir singing recessional hymn.)

(DAISY *exits house left.)*

(Procession forms and exits up stage right.)

END OF PLAY

www.ingramcontent.com/pod-product-compliance
Lightning Source LLC
Chambersburg PA
CBHW070028110426
42741CB00034B/2679